Don't know just yet

Neus Ferrer

BookLeaf
Publishing

Don't know just yet © 2022 Neus Ferrer

All rights reserved.

No part of this publication may be reproduced, stored in a retrieval system, or transmitted, in any form or by any means, electronic, mechanical, photocopying, recording or otherwise, without the prior written permission of the presenters.

Neus Ferrer asserts the moral right to be identified as author of this work.

Presentation by *BookLeaf Publishing*

Web: www.bookleafpub.com

E-mail: info@bookleafpub.com

ISBN: 9789357695985

First edition 2022

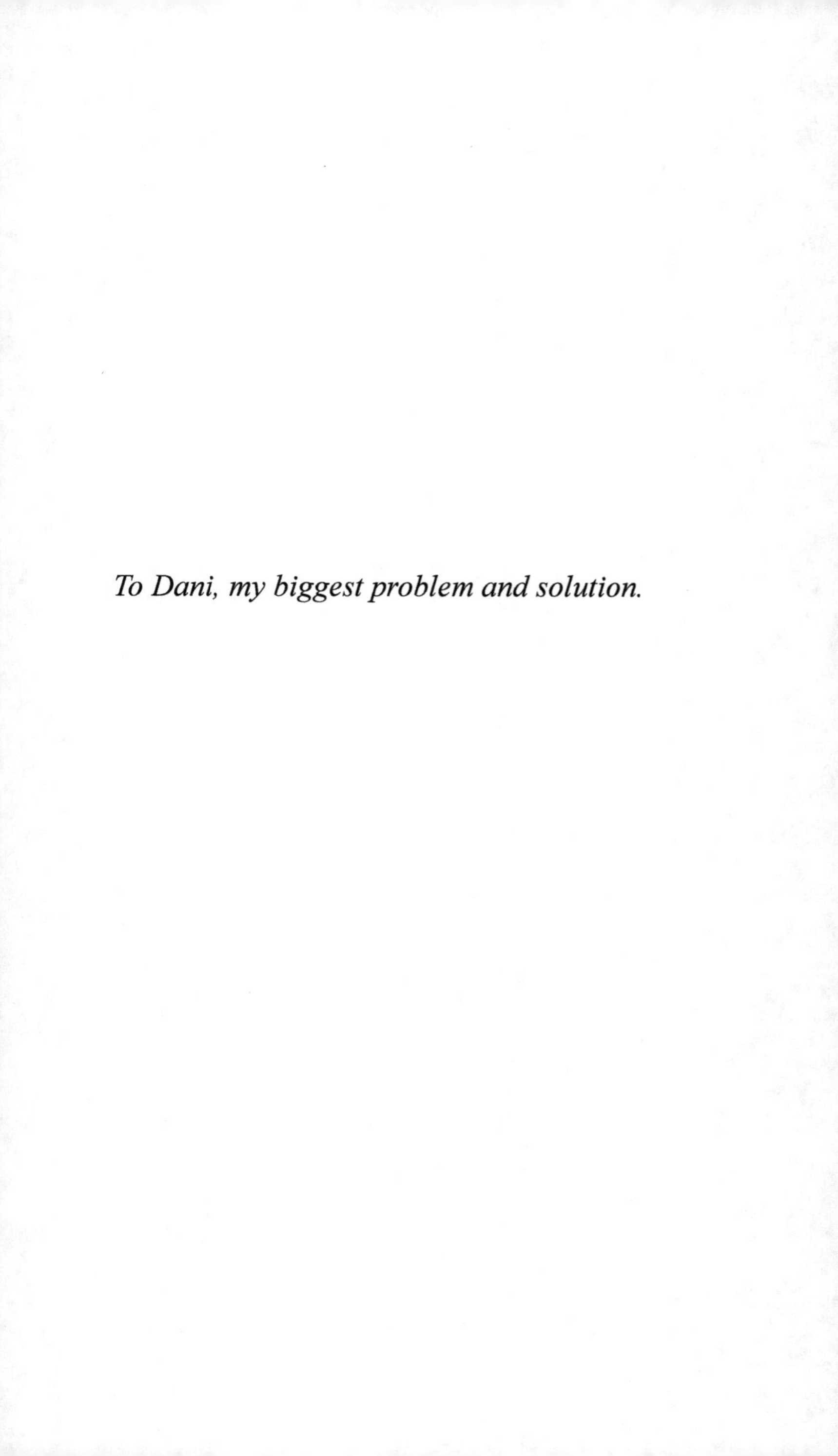

To Dani, my biggest problem and solution.

Dawdle

Papers full of scribbles, jotting,
never happened.
Masters degree in Goldsmiths,
never happened.
Live art projects sketched in half empty
handmade notebooks.
Pictures and videos cramming my smartphone.
Unread art books lying on my shelves,
cramping me.

Dawdling away since 2012

Wake up

Woke up to see that
everything has changed.

I used to oversleep,
to watch the sunrise dancing,
to believe in modern fairy tales and
dream with the unreachable.

I used to burn my skin
with your soft and long fingers,
thinking that there is no other place I would
rather be.
Floating in a cloudy nada.

But now everything has changed.

I wake up before sunrise waddling my way to
the stove kitchen.
Uncertain if I'll be able to fill the coffee maker
with this little coffee left.

I am still thirsty
for your warm and tight hug,
but your fingers don't burn my already melted
skin,

while I am wishing for the time to stop
to permanently breathe

the nothingness of this void.

Frustration

It comes in different shapes and sizes.
For me it is a wave that crawls
from my stomach
to the top of my head
it bubbles its way up to the top,
filling up everything
turning into a blurry veil.

Oh, gosh if only I could see something when this
happens!

Blindly feeling.
I don't run anymore.
I stand under the heavy rain.
I don't care if stops or not.
Charging my words
as if they were a gun.

Bam bang bang!
Energy outburst.
Powercut.

Anger

5

Don't lose your temper!

Tells me with a smile on his face...

Darling, that is a very big thing to ask
to someone with suspected borderline
personality disorder.
At night,
somewhere around 2 a.m
I am a Google doctor.

No worries.

Nothing catchy.

Very painful to bear though.

One by one

An outsider.
Never fitting in.
Is it all in my mind?
Yesterday the world was going to collapse,
today it seems that things are not that bad.

Changing with the wind
as a weather vane
going against the wind
would be fighting in vane.
What if I can't stop pushing for the other side?
What if I AM quite ready for the flight?
But is it not like that how everyone works?
I lost my mind somewhere at the docks?
 I am crazy or they are.
Sailing in all directions I can't read a radar.
Throw me your stones
with them
I will build my wall.

One by one.

Morning battles

Once again.
Here I am 4.47 a.m.
39 years old.
Never imagined that my body could hurt
the way it does.

Hinges creak
squeaking mice
hammer thumps,
it is hitting so hard
that my brittle laugh
can break in at any time
now.

Trying to grow some backbone
to grow a spine
to make some good choices...
Don't let them walk all over you
THEM! WHO'S THEM?
Sit up nicely.
Stand up.
Speak up.
Have courage.
Do the right thing.
Be an example.

A role model.
Don't let THEM tear you down.
OH, THEM AGAIN!

Follow your instincts.
Be a person of high morals.
(Crumbling down at this point)
Never cease giving a good example.

Show your power.
Step up your game.
Cut it out!
a pressure cooker
about to explode.

A hard beast to tame.

Unbearable

Not possible.
I look into your eyes and
where I once saw the ocean
now is a paddle.
Unbelievable, shallow.

Your love that I once thought a cliff
is the step into my house.
Wooden flooring, hollow,
unfortunately eaten by woodworm.

I can hear it munching
until it is reduced to zero.

Uncertainly broken.
I cannot think clearly
and your smile all of a sudden
lights up everything.
Makes me feel sad
that I couldn't see it before the storm.
Before the Armaggedon.

I, you, us is that still a thing?
Something stings.
My sanity is hanging on a string.

Just happen to know

Happened before,
will happen again.
I just can't stay until the end
watching.

Happened before,
not happening again.
My head spinning.
My heart hurting.
My eyes pumping.

Happened before,
I should see it coming.
I don't fit anymore in my skin
which I never felt like mine anyway,
uncapable of undestanding how you cannot see
it at all...

Why are you still trying to make a point.
Why are we still trying to make it work.
Why I am still banging my head against the
wall.
Why are you still believing in...
Not even sure what you believe in anymore.
I am not sure what you want to pull out.

Not convinced of the point that you want to
prove.
I guess I'll have to wait and see,to watch till the
end,
to sit patiently until the credits finish.
And the lights are on.

Seismic waves

Let me play with the sound
of the ocean,
I would rather die 10 times than miss it.

Only once more,
until my world starts shaking again
and I lose the little faith that I had in me.

There's something in boring routines,
despite the word boring
they are pleasant, sought-after
the stability of the known.

1.9 Ritcher scale.

Boring is the word that should be out of the
equation.
It crawls behind my back
ruining the peace
and my world starts to shake again.

4.5 Richter scale.

Please let me smell behind your ear
the place were your neck is soft and warm.

Let me feel the calm before the storm
to navigate this last moment
before all this is gone.

8.0 Richter scale.

And then all will be silent.

Middle of the road

I' ve got stuck on the middle bit
of life.
Still didn't figure out what to do.
Without the flexibility of being young.
Middle age,
where successful people sits enjoying the fruits
of their labour.
Middle finger.
Tired of the whinging.
I don't see how this can be solved.
Angry at the "this is normal"
"It will pass"
"Oh, thats nothing"
NO IT ISN'T!

Raging love switched to raging
in the middle of the night.
Awake.
Again.
Again.
Whining.
Inaproppriate feeling.
Sit next to me,
I am lost in the middle of the road
again.

Together we will endure.
Under our arms tangled in a hug.
The winds and the hail and the heavy rains.
And we will make it in one piece.

Don't be scared
I'll always be there
for the both of us.
But be aware,
I am not sure
if this is more of a promise
or a threat.
And sliding outside
from under our shelter
bright skies will welcome us
to the golden age.

Don't be afraid.
Boredom only hits once.
And we are way over that.

Should I have?

I went straight for it and gosh,
let me tell you that probably
I should
definitely have not.
Now that it's done
let's enjoy the ride.
Something to hide?
Should we wait till 12 o'clock ?
so we make sure
you are not a pumpkin
and I am really made of gold.
It took you some time to reach me
but hey-ho
here I am
take it all.

Today

Trying to reach.
To feel with my fingertips

the wall.

Complaints

Be quiet.
Starts the nightmare.
I am holding on to the handrail
as hard as I can.
Silent please.
In crescendo, the anger.
And you're still talking.
¡Cállate!
 a letany.
A miserable recital
sorrowful and nonsensical.
Makes me feel sick.
My stomach can't have it for much longer...
My train is gone.

When

When was the last time that I walked carelessly
on the street?
When did I lost the spontaneity?
When did I started quoting my parents?
When it was the last time that I slept alone?
Which was the last book I read in one go?
Which were those sweets that I liked so much?
When did I stopped to feel my body mine?
When did I gave up of trying to remember phone
numbers and birthdays dates?
When did a pint started to be one to many?
How many days have passed without sleeping?
When was the last time I was on my own?
How on earth did I lose the ability to jump on
things?
When did procrastination was the new habit to
break?
What kind of torture is this?

Weekends

I wish the weekend was longuer
I wish it had five days at least.
Everyone would say the same
You are thinking
How original!
You would say
I will tell you no.
It was not always was like this.

Nothing to lose.
Nothing to gain.
Coming from a dark place.
Going to a darker one.
Listening to the crows singing my name.
Birds in my mane.
A dandelion to tame.
With a melodious voice.
Calling me from beyond.
To shout at me after, with a thousand voices.
Deafening me.

I could not shed a tear.
Not a drop of water passing through my throat.
Loneliness.
Emptiness.

Sorrowful to my best.

No it wasn't always like this.

Lost in transit, traffic and translation.
Not understanding a single number of the
equation.
Crawling at day.
At night floating.
Forgetting who I was if
I ever was something.

Numbers

The order of the factors does not alter the
product.
Less is zero.
Everything around us is numbers
and maths wasn't my strongest subject.
I could count with the fingers on my hands
all the times I missed the opportunity
but still,
I will always choose you
over all the population,
in a hundred lives.

Countdown.

23

No time to lose,
1% battery.

Time is gone

and I don't not just yet.

www.ingramcontent.com/pod-product-compliance
Lightning Source LLC
La Vergne TN
LVHW021348200726
843509LV00014B/2727